SCIENCE OF FUN STUFF

The Innings and Outs of Baseball

by Jordan D. Brown
illustrated by Dagney Downey

Ready-to-Read

Simon Spotlight
New York   London   Toronto   Sydney   New Delhi

SIMON SPOTLIGHT
An imprint of Simon & Schuster Children's Publishing Division
1230 Avenue of the Americas, New York, New York 10020
This Simon Spotlight edition September 2016
Text copyright © 2015 by Simon & Schuster Inc.
Illustrations copyright © 2015 by Dagney Downey
For information about special discounts for bulk purchases, please contact Simon & Schuster Special Sales at
1-866-506-1949 or business@simonandschuster.com.
The Simon & Schuster Speakers Bureau can bring authors to your live event. For more information or to
book an event contact the Simon & Schuster Speakers Bureau at 1-866-248-3049 or visit our
website at www.simonspeakers.com.
Manufactured in China 0417 SDI

CONTENTS

CHAPTER 1
It's a Hit!

Baseball stadiums are wonderful places for amazing athletes, screaming fans, and curious scientists. "Whoa!" you say. "What does science have to do with baseball?" As you'll see, baseball is *bursting* with science. What are the secrets for hitting a home run? What makes a curveball curve? And how do pro players get grass stains out of their uniforms? Science can answer all these questions and more. Now let's play ball!

Your baseball dream is about to come true. As you step up to the plate the stadium is filled with fans. The score is tied and the bases are loaded. The ball hurls at you at 90 miles an hour—and *CRACK!*—you hit a home run! As you bask in the glory, you wonder: What made the ball travel so far?

NEWTON

POW

More than 300 years ago, a science genius named Sir Isaac Newton discovered three rules for how things move. His First Law of Motion says that moving objects will keep moving—in the same direction and at the same speed—until a force slows them. When a baseball is hit, it flies through the air until it is pulled down by Earth's gravity.

Gravity is a force that pulls all objects toward one another. Newton figured out that very big things (like our planet) have WAY more gravitational pull than small things (like a baseball). If Earth's gravity were suddenly turned off after a batter hit a ball, it could travel into outer space!

Another force that slows down a baseball is drag. Drag is a type of friction. When a ball moves through the air, the air rubs against it. This is because air is filled with tiny molecules that push the ball. A spinning ball's stitches add to drag, and help it fight gravity. In fact, if a baseball didn't have stitches, hitting a home run wouldn't be possible.

Newton's Second Law of Motion says that the more force that is put on an object, the more the object will accelerate, or speed up. So the harder a baseball is hit, the greater its speed. The amount of motion an object has is called momentum. The more momentum something has, the harder it is to stop it.

I GOT IT!

That's why, with a home run, the ball is going . . . going . . . gone.

Newton's Third Law says that for every action, there is a reaction. When a batter hits the ball (the action), the swing stops the ball, and then pushes it back (the reaction).

Don't worry if Newton's Laws are making your head spin. They can take years to master. (If Newton were alive, he might joke, "See? My ideas making your head spin is proof of my Third Law!")

To hit a home run, batters usually hit the ball on the "sweet spot," about 6 inches from the end of the bat.

SWEET SPOT

What makes the "sweet spot" hit so powerful? When a bat hits the ball, the bat vibrates, or shakes back and forth. If the bat vibrates a lot, the hit is not as strong. But hitting the sweet spot causes the fewest vibrations. That means more of the ball's energy is transferred into hitting the ball away.

ANOTHER SWEET SPOT?

Speaking of bats, they are not all made of the same stuff. As you may know, some bats are wooden and others are made of metal. But which kind of bat can hit a ball farther? Aluminum bats can. One reason is that they are lighter. So, you can swing them faster than wooden ones.

On a hot day, players can have sweaty palms. When this happens, they have a harder time gripping the bat, which slows down their swinging speed. That's why many players rub pine tar on the handle of their bats before the game. This sticky stuff, from pine trees, keeps their hands from slipping.

CHAPTER 2
Tricky Pitches

Hitters and pitchers may seem like opposites, but they have the same goal: They both want to move the baseball quickly. Hitters use a bat, while pitchers use special tricks to control the ball. Hitters and pitchers want to fight the forces of physics—the science of motion and energy.

What forces affect a pitcher's throw? As soon as a ball leaves a pitcher's hand, gravity pulls it downward. The ball is also slowed down by drag as it flies to home plate. Even the ball's 108 stiches add to the drag.

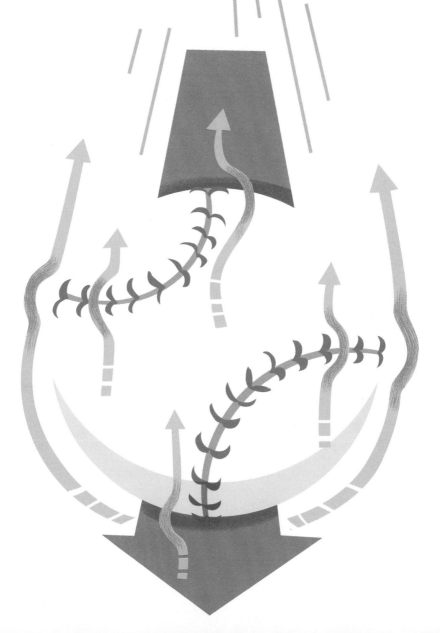

To fight gravity and drag, pitchers build up energy by doing "windups." Before releasing the ball, they step back, twist their body, and move their weight to their back leg. They hold the ball as far back as possible. Then, as they throw, they switch their weight forward. What is the science behind all this movement?

Remember Newton's First Law? It says that moving objects "like" to keep moving. Well, the opposite is also true. Newton found that still objects "like" to stay put. So, to give the ball energy and build momentum, the pitcher winds up.

THE
4
SEAM
FASTBALL

To fight gravity, a pitcher often puts spin on the ball. This controls the way air moves around it, which makes it move in surprising ways. One tricky pitch is the fastball. In this pitch, the pitcher puts "backspin" on the ball which causes "lift," a force that fights gravity.

THE 2 SEAM FASTBALL

When a fastball moves at more than 100 miles per hour, it is very hard to hit. To throw a fastball, a pitcher uses a special grip and holds the ball as loosely as possible. The loose grip reduces friction, so it leaves the hand quickly.

Then there's the curveball. It looks like it's headed straight for home plate, but then arcs downward near home plate. To throw a curveball, the pitcher snaps his wrist in a turning motion. This gives the ball "topspin," which makes the air under the ball flow faster than the air on top of the ball.

This air flow creates less pressure around the ball, so it drops downward. Known as the "Magnus Force," the spinning air around a baseball can change its path. Scientists have studied curveballs using high-speed cameras and wind tunnels. Wind tunnels are tubes that have air blowing through them.

Another tricky pitch is the knuckleball. Unlike the fastball and the curveball, when a pitcher throws a knuckleball, it has no spin on it. Without spin, a hurling ball creates lots of drag, and the ball moves all over the place.

No matter what pitch is thrown, all baseballs are made of the same materials. The center, called "the pill," is made of cork and rubber. Wound around the pill are layers of wool and rubber. The outside is covered with adhesive and leather, which is stitched with red thread.

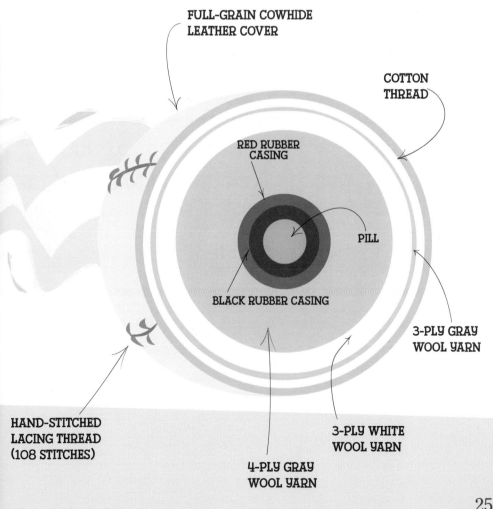

FULL-GRAIN COWHIDE
LEATHER COVER

COTTON
THREAD

RED RUBBER
CASING

PILL

BLACK RUBBER CASING

3-PLY GRAY
WOOL YARN

HAND-STITCHED
LACING THREAD
(108 STITCHES)

3-PLY WHITE
WOOL YARN

4-PLY GRAY
WOOL YARN

CHAPTER 3
Baseball Experiments

Scientists sometimes study baseball in a lab. In 2006, scientists at Washington University in St. Louis wanted to learn why home-run superstar Albert Pujols was such an amazing hitter. First, they hooked him up to a machine to measure his batting speed. He swung the bat at 86.99 miles per hour!

The scientists also wanted to study Pujols's "reaction times"—how fast his eyes move. They used a special video camera to measure how fast his eyes moved from one place to another. They found that his reaction times were about 16-18 milliseconds faster than most people's. That's a lot when you consider how quickly the average pitch travels from pitcher to catcher.

To study the speed of Pujols's muscles, the scientists asked him to tap his finger on a machine as many times as possible in 10 seconds. He tapped so fast that he tapped the machine out of alignment! These experiments help to explain some of the reasons why Albert Pujols is such an exceptional hitter.

Scientists have even created robots to help them understand how pro ballplayers do their thing. At the University of Toyko in Japan, they built a robot that uses its three-fingered hand to pitch a ball. It succeeds at hitting the strike zone 90 percent of the time! Another robot they built uses high-tech sensors to bat a ball almost every time.

ALTITUDE...

5000 FT.

Scientists have found that altitude can affect how far a hit will travel. For example, a home run hit in a high-altitude stadium in Denver, Colorado, will go about 40 feet farther than if it were hit in a low-altitude stadium in New York City. This is because the air is thinner in high places, so there's less drag.

Sometimes attitude is even more important than altitude. Yogi Berra, a New York Yankee, once said, "Baseball is 90 percent mental. The other half is physical." Berra's math is obviously a joke, but his point is 100 percent accurate. Scientists have found that how players think affects their playing.

CHAPTER 4
The Stadium Experience

Before the fans arrive, groundskeepers at stadiums spend many hours getting things ready. Have you ever wondered how they create checkerboard patterns on the field? It looks like they use two different-colored grasses, but they don't. Instead, they use the science of optics, a type of physics that studies light.

To fool your eyes to see the pattern, they use a flat roller to press down some stripes of grass. This way, the blades of grass that are bent away from you reflect more sunlight, so they appear lighter green. The blades that stand straight reflect less sunlight, so they look darker.

Speaking of grass, how do pro players get all those nasty stains out of their uniforms? Removing all the grass, dirt, sweat, and blood stains can be a challenge. Luckily, "clubbies," the guys who work in the clubhouse, understand the science of stain removal. They know that grass stains are caused by chlorophyll, a green dye found in many plants.

Clubbies use special detergents for removing stains. These detergents use chemistry to pull out the stains. Normally, water molecules stick to one another. This stickiness, called "surface tension," can make stains hard to remove. But the soap in detergents lowers the water's surface tension, which helps the stains come out in the soapy water.

Grass-stained uniforms aren't the only problem that occurs at stadiums. At big games, fans have to deal with sound difficulties. Sometimes the announcer's voice echoes or the stadium becomes so noisy that you can't hear your neighbor.

The science of how sound travels in a large space is called "acoustics." Most of the sounds we hear are vibrations in the air. Our ears pick up these sound vibrations and send them to our brains. In ballparks, the sound waves bounce off the walls, making it difficult to hear. To help solve the problem, they sometimes put padding and banners in places that help absorb the sound.

While our ears can become overwhelmed by stadium sounds, our noses can face a similar dilemma. Our sense of smell sniffs out all those delicious hot dogs, warm pretzels, and fries. How does your nose smell your favorite baseball stadium snacks?

Everything that smells gives off tiny scent molecules. When you smell the air, these molecules travel into your nose. Inside your nose, there are millions of special odor cells that pick up the molecules. When these cells send a message to your brain, it tells you, "Ohh, a hot dog! I want one."

SCIENCE
OF
FUN STUFF
EXPERT
ON
BASEBALL

Congratulations! You've just made it to home plate. You are now an official Science of Fun Stuff Expert on baseball. Impress your friends and family with all the cool things you know about the physics of pitching. And the next time you go to a baseball game, or play yourself, don't forget the science behind the swings.

Hey, kids! Now that you're an expert on the science of baseball, turn the page to learn even more about this classic sport and some social studies, history, and anatomy along the way!

Baseball Timeline

A timeline is a great way to illustrate a set of historical events. The events on a timeline usually follow a theme or take place within a specific period of time.

To make a timeline, first create a list of events you want to include and order them chronologically (that's a fancy way of saying earliest to latest). Then look at your earliest and latest event dates to determine the period your timeline will cover. The earliest date goes at the left end of the timeline, while the latest date goes on the right.

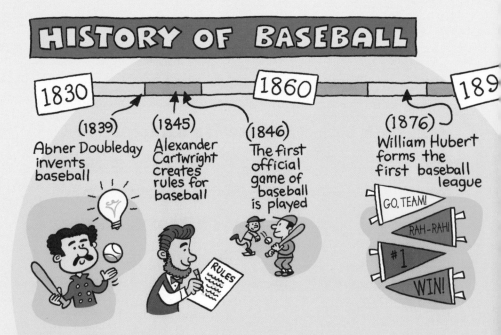

HISTORY OF BASEBALL

1830   1860   189

(1839) Abner Doubleday invents baseball

(1845) Alexander Cartwright creates rules for baseball

(1846) The first official game of baseball is played

(1876) William Hubert forms the first baseball league

RULES

GO, TEAM!
RAH-RAH!
#1
WIN!

Now split the timeline into segments by drawing smaller, intersecting lines at equal lengths apart. Each line represents a unit of time; a unit can be a day, a month, a year, or even a hundred years! Label every few units with the year it represents on the timeline.

Now add your list of events to the timeline, marking them at the corresponding year. You can make a timeline about anything—the events of your favorite TV show, the founding of the United States, even the history of baseball. . . .

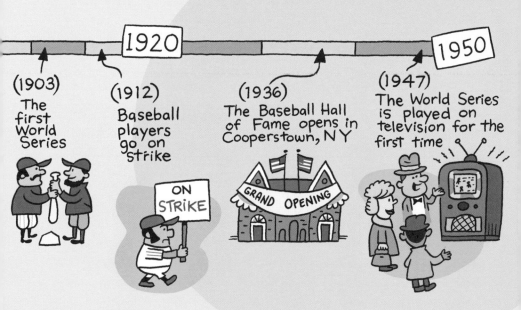

1920   1950

(1903)
The first World Series

(1912)
Baseball players go on strike

ON STRIKE

(1936)
The Baseball Hall of Fame opens in Cooperstown, NY

GRAND OPENING

(1947)
The World Series is played on television for the first time

Women in Baseball

Many people may think baseball is a boy's game, but girls have been playing America's favorite pastime since the 1860s. Check out these feisty female players who showed that they could hold their own against baseball's best any day!

Alta Weiss: In 1907, after striking out 15 men, Alta Weiss signed with the semiprofessional Vermilion Independents, an otherwise all-male team.

Jackie Mitchell: In 1931, Jackie Mitchell signed a contract with the Minor League Chattanooga Lookouts, making her the first female professional baseball player. Mitchell went on to play an exhibition game against the Yankees, where, at just 17 years old, she struck out both Babe Ruth and Lou Gehrig!

Toni Stone: Toni Stone became the first woman to play professionally in a men's league when she signed with the Indianapolis Clowns in 1953, replacing none other than Hank Aaron at second base. She appeared in 50 games that year and even played with Willie Mays!

Ila Borders: In 1997, Ila Borders became the first woman to pitch in a Minor League baseball game. The following year, Borders claimed another title: first woman to get a win in a professional game!

Eri Yoshida: At only 18 years old in 2010, Eri Yoshida was the first woman to play professionally in 2 countries, having pitched in an independent league in Japan as well as in the United States. The press dubbed her the "knuckle princess" for her incredible pitches.

Twist My Arm!
The Anatomy of the Arm

Anatomy is the study of the structure of the human body, including the bones, muscles, and joints. Pitching a fastball may look easy, but on the inside, many parts of the body are working together.

A joint is any place in the body where two or more bones meet. Because our bones are rigid, but we still need to bend so we can walk, jump, and move, joints allow our body to bend without breaking bones. Let's take a closer look at some of the joints of the arm, which play a huge role in pitching.

The finger joints that wrap around the ball are known as "hinge" joints because they only move in two directions, like the hinges that help a door to open and close.

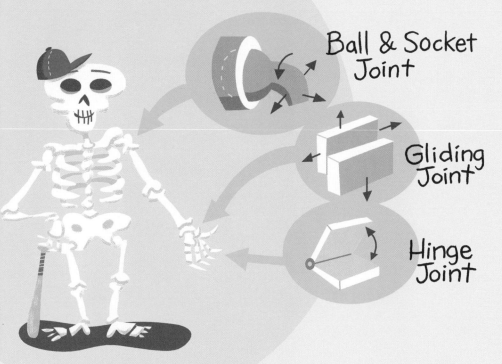

Ball & Socket Joint

Gliding Joint

Hinge Joint

The wrist, which often determines the type of pitch, is a "gliding" joint. Gliding joints are made up of many smaller bones that glide past one another. Gliding joints are usually found on flat surfaces of the body, such as the wrists and palms.

Your shoulder that winds up the pitch is a "ball and socket" joint. Ball and socket joints have two parts: a bone with a rounded head and a bone that looks like a cup. The cup bone fits around the ball bone, allowing you to move your arm up, down, left, right, inward, and outward.

So give your joints a hand: They're working hard to help you pitch your next no-hitter!

Being an expert on something means you can get an awesome score on a quiz on that subject! Take this

SCIENCE OF BASEBALL QUIZ

to see how much you've learned.

1. What force pulls a baseball down to Earth as it flies through the air?

   a. Gravity   b. Tomatoes   c. Lift

2. Drag is a type of what force?

   a. Speed   b. Gravity   c. Friction

3. According to Newton's Second Law of Motion, the more force that is put on an object, the more it will . . .

   a. Slow Down   b. Speed Up   c. Stay the Same

4. Which kind of bat can hit a ball farther: wood or aluminum?

   a. Wood   b. Aluminum   c. Both Hit the Same Distance

5. Physics is the science of motion and what else?

   a. Chemicals   b. Energy   c. Sausages

6. To fight gravity, a pitcher often puts what on a ball?

   a. Spin   b. Salsa   c. Weight

7. Why do players hold a fastball as loosely as possible when they pitch?

   a. To Increase Drag   b. It's a Rule   c. To Reduce Friction

8. Curveballs rely on what to make the ball curve?

   a. Topspin   b. Batters   c. Gravity

9. Why are knuckleballs unique?

   a. They Have No Spin   b. They Have Less Drag   c. They Go Straight

10. Because the air is thinner in high places, there is less what?

   a. Energy   b. Hot Dogs   c. Drag

Answers: 1.a 2.c 3.b 4.b 5.b 6.a 7.c 8.a 9.a 10.c